WOMEN OF THE SPIRIT

BIBLE STUDY

Vol. VI: THE POWER OF PRAISE

JOY HANEY

All Scripture quotations are from the King James Version of the Holy Bible unless otherwise noted.

Women of the Spirit Bible Study by Joy Haney
Volume VI: The Power of Praise
Published by Radiant Life Publications
Stockton, California
First Printing April, 1996
Copyright © April, 1996

Printed in the United States of America

Library of Congress Catalog Number 94-68446
ISBN # 1-880969-25-4

Introduction

May the *Women of the Spirit Volume VI: The Power of Praise,* be the blessing to you that it was to me while writing it.

On February 23,1996, the Lord awakened me at 2:30 a.m. and impressed me to read the entire Book of Psalms. While reading it, I began to praise the Lord, and became so blessed that tears started running down my cheeks. My soul felt so close to God. My emotions were deeply stirred with a heightened awareness of the glory of God and the power and excellency of praise.

It is my desire to obey Psalm 26:7, which says, "That I may publish with the voice of thanksgiving, and tell of all thy wondrous works."

Women of the Spirit Bible Study
Volume VI: The Power of Praise

Contents

Lessons:

Women of the Spirit Bible Study

Lesson I

I. PRAISE YE THE LORD

A. Definition of Praise is as follows:

    1. Praise means to glorify God by homage.

        a. Homage means respect, reverential regard, or obeisance.

        b. Glorify means to make glorious by bestowing glory upon, or to magnify in worship; to adore and exalt.

        c. Obeisance means submission or reverence.

    2. Praise means to magnify (especially in song), extol, acclaim or to express approval.

B. Antonym of praise is blame.

    1. To blame God instead of praising God is a sin.

        a. Job 2:10 says, "But he said unto her, Thou speakest as one of the foolish women speaketh. What? shall we receive good at the hand of God and shall we not receive evil? In all this did not Job sin with his lips."

b. What did Job do instead of blaming God for his misfortune? Job 1:20-22 says the following:

   i.   *Verse 20*: "Then Job arose, and rent his mantle, and shaved his head, and fell down upon the ground, and worshipped."

   ii. *Verse21*: "And said, naked came I out of my mother's womb, and naked shall I return thither: the LORD gave, and the LORD hath taken away; blessed be the name of the LORD."

   iii. *Verse 22:* "In all this Job sinned not, nor charged God foolishly."

c. Psalm 59:12 says, "For the sin of their mouth and the words of their lips let them even be taken in their pride: and for cursing and lying which they speak."

2. Cursing instead of praising is displeasing to God.

   a. Read James 3:9-11

      i.   *Verse 9*: "Therewith bless we God, even the Father; and therewith curse we men, which are made after the similitude of God."

      ii. *Verse 10*: "Out of the same mouth proceedeth blessing and cursing. My brethren, these things ought not so to be."

      iii. *Verse 11*: "Doth a fountain send forth at the same place sweet water and bitter?"

   b. Leviticus 24:14-16 demonstrates how strongly God wants us to bless His name and not curse it.

        i.   *Verse 14*: "Bring forth him that hath cursed without the camp; and let all that heard him lay hands upon his head, and let all the congregation stone him."

        ii.   *Verse 15*: "And thou shalt speak unto the children of Israel, saying, Whosoever curseth his God shall bear his sin."

        iii.   *Verse 16*: "And he that blasphemeth the name of the LORD, he shall surely be put to death, and all the congregation shall certainly stone him: as well the stranger, as he that is born in the land, when he blaphemeth the name of the LORD, shall be put to death."

C.   We are commanded to praise the LORD. Please read the following Scriptures:

    1.   "Praise ye the LORD, Blessed is the man that feareth the LORD, that delighteth greatly in his commandments" (Psalm 112:1).

    2.   "Praise ye the LORD, Praise O ye servants of the LORD, praise the name of the LORD. Blessed be the name of the LORD from this time forth and for evermore. From the rising of the sun unto the going down of the same the LORD'S name is to be praised" (Psalm 113:1-3).

    3.   "O praise the LORD, all ye nations: praise him, all ye people" (Psalm 117:1).

    4.   "Praise ye the LORD. Praise the LORD, O my soul. While I live will I praise the LORD: I will sing praises unto my God while I have any being" (Psalm 146:1-2).

5.   "Praise ye the LORD: for it is good to sing praises unto our God; for it is pleasant; and praise is comely" (Psalm147:1).

6.   "Praise ye the LORD. Praise ye the LORD from the heavens: praise him in the heights" (Psalm 148:1).

D.   Our purpose in life is to show forth His praises and to glorify Him.

1.   I Peter 2:9 says, "But ye are a chosen generation, a royal priesthood, an holy nation, a peculiar people; that ye should show forth the praises of him who hath called you out of darkness into his marvellous light:"

2.   Psalm 107:1-2 says, "O GIVE thanks unto the LORD, for he is good: for his mercy endureth for ever. Let the redeemed of the LORD say so, whom he hath redeemed from the hand of the enemy;"

3.   Psalm 22:26 says, "The meek shall eat and be satisfied: they shall praise the LORD that seek him: your heart shall live for ever."

E.   It is the LORD's very strong desire that people would praise Him.

1.   Notice in Psalm 107, the four verses that are identical. They begin with the word "Oh" and end with an exclamation point. An exclamation point indicates forceful utterance or strong feeling.

2.   Psalm 107:8, 15, 21,31 speak the same forceful words. "Oh that men would praise the LORD for his goodness, and for his wonderful works to the children of men!"

F.   He dwells with and surrounds those who praise Him.

    1.   Psalm 22:3 says, "But thou art holy, O thou that inhabitest the praises of Israel." He makes his abode in the praises of His people. Praise is where God dwells.

    2.   Please read Psalm 67:3-5

        a.   *Verse 3*: "Let the people praise thee, O God: let all the people praise thee."

        b.   *Verse 4*: "O let the nations be glad and sing for joy: for thou shalt judge the people righteously, and govern the nations upon earth. Selah."

        c.   *Verse 5*: "Let the people praise thee, O God; let all the people praise thee."

    3.   Notice Psalm 67:6-7. This is the *result* of praise.

        a.   *Verse 6*: "Then shall the earth yield her increase; and God, even our own God, shall bless us."

        b.   *Verse 7*: "God shall bless us; and all the ends of the earth shall fear him."

    4.   The glory of the Lord filled the house *after* they praised Him.

        a.   II Chronicles 5:13-14 says, "It came even to pass, as the trumpeters and singers were as one, to make one sound to be heard in praising and thanking the LORD; and when they lifted up their voice with the trumpets and cymbals and instruments of music, and praised the LORD, saying, For he is good; for his mercy endureth for ever: that then the house was filled with a cloud, even the house of the LORD; So that the priests could not stand to minister by reason of the cloud: for the glory of the LORD had filled the house of God."

    b.   Notice the phrase *then the house was filled with a cloud*. The glory came after the praise.

G.   We are commanded to enter His courts with praise.

    1.   Psalm 100:4 says, "Enter into his gates with thanksgiving, and into his courts with praise: be thankful unto him, and bless his name."

    2.   The court represents the place where the Lord visits His people. Ezekiel 10:3-5 demonstrates what happens when worship is given to God almighty.

        a.   Notice, as the cherubims worshipped, the glory came.

        b.   *Verse 3*: "Now the cherubims stood on the right side of the house, when the man went in; and the cloud filled the inner court."

        c.   *Verse 4*: "Then the glory of the LORD went up from the cherub, and stood over the threshold of the house; and the house was filled with the cloud, and the court was full of the brightness of the Lord's glory."

        d.   *Verse 5*: "And the sound of the cherubims' wings was heard even to the outer court, as the voice of the Almighty God when he speaketh."

H.   We are to praise Him even when we are around unsaved people.

    1.   Psalm 18:49 says, "Therefore will I give thanks unto thee, O LORD, among the heathen, and sing praises unto thy name."

2.   Psalm 96:3 says, "Declare his glory among the heathen, his wonders among all people."

J.   We are to praise Him when we are with other Christians.

1.   Psalm 22:22 says, "I will declare thy name unto my brethren: in the midst of the congregation will I praise thee."

2.   Psalm 22:25 says, "My praise shall be of thee in the great congregation: I will pay my vows before them that fear him."

3.   Psalm 35:18 says, "I will give thee thanks in the great congregation: I will praise thee among much people."

K.   Praise is referred to as a sacrifice.

1.   Psalm 54:6 says, "I will freely sacrifice unto thee: I will praise thy name, O LORD; for it is good."

2.   Hebrews 13:15 says, "By him therefore let us offer the sacrifice of praise to God continually, that is, the fruit of our lips giving thanks to his name."

3.   Psalm 61:8 says, "So will I sing praise unto thy name for ever, that I may daily perform my vows."

4.   Psalm 96:8 says, "Give unto the LORD the glory due unto his name: bring an offering, and come into his courts."

5.   Psalm 56:12 says, "Thy vows are upon me, O God: I will render praises unto thee."

L.   Praise Him because of His marvelous works.

    1.   Psalm 139:14 says, "I will praise thee; for I am fearfully and wonderfully made: marvellous are thy works; and that my soul knoweth right well."

    2.   Psalm 118:23,24,28 says, "This is the LORD's doing; it is marvellous in our eyes. This is the day which the LORD hath made; we will rejoice and be glad in it. Thou art my God, and I will praise thee: thou art my God, I will exalt thee."

    3.   I Chronicles 16:29 says, "Give unto the LORD the glory due unto his name: bring an offering, and come before him: worship the LORD in the beauty of holiness."

M.   God deserves our praise because He is good and worthy.

    1.   Psalm 29:2 says, "Give unto the LORD the glory due unto his name; worship the LORD in the beauty of holiness."

    2.   Psalm 106:1 says, "Praise ye the LORD. O give thanks unto the LORD; for he is good: for his mercy endureth for ever."

    3.   Psalm 18:3 says, "I will call upon the Lord, who is worthy to be praised: so shall I be saved from mine enemies."

    4.   I Chronicles 16:20 says, "Give unto the LORD the glory due unto his name: bring an offering and come before him: worship the LORD in the beauty of holiness."

N.   Praise His WORD.

    1.   Psalm 56:4 says, "In God I will praise his word, in God I have put my trust; I will not fear what flesh can do unto me."

2.   Psalm 56:10 says, "In God will I praise his word: in the LORD will I praise his word."

3.   Psalm 138:2 says, "I will worship toward thy holy temple, and praise thy name for thy lovingkindness and for thy truth: for thou hast magnified thy word above all thy name."

Lesson I Quiz

1.	Give the definition of praise.

2.	What is the antonym of praise?

3.	Write the following Scriptures from memory:

	a.	*I Peter 2:9*:

	b.	*Psalm 107:8, 15, 21, 31* (all the same):

	c.	*Psalm 139:14*:

	d.	*I Chronicles 16:29*:

4.	Give the time the glory filled the house in II Chronicles 5:13-14.

5.	How are we commanded to enter His presence? Give scriptural reference.

6.	Praise is referred to as what? Give scriptural reference.

7.	Are God's children *commanded* to praise Him? Give scriptural reference.

Women of the Spirit Bible Study

*Rejoice and
Shout for Joy*

Lesson II

II. REJOICE AND SHOUT FOR JOY

A. Those who put their trust in God are instructed to rejoice and shout for joy.

    1. Psalm 5:11 says, "But let all those that put their trust in thee rejoice: let them ever shout for joy, because thou defendest them: let them also that love thy name be joyful in thee."

    2. Psalm 33:21 says, " For our heart shall rejoice in him, because we have trusted in his holy name."

B. The upright are instructed to be glad and shout.

    1. Psalm 32:11 says, "Be glad in the LORD, and rejoice, ye righteous: and shout for joy, all ye that are upright in heart."

    2. Psalm 33:1 says, "Rejoice in the LORD, O ye righteous: for praise is comely for the upright."

        a. Comely means beautiful.

        b. Upright means to be morally correct, honest, and just.

3. Psalm 64:10 says, "The righteous shall be glad in the LORD, and shall trust in him; and all the upright in heart shall glory."

C. When your mouth is filled with joy and laughter, you are testifying of God's glory.

1. Psalm 126:1-2 says, "When the LORD turned again the captivity of Zion, we were like them that dream. Then was our mouth filled with laughter, and our tongue with singing: then said they among the heathen, The LORD hath done great things for them."

2. Psalm 63:5 says, "My soul shall be satisfied as with marrow and fatness; and my mouth shall praise thee with joyful lips:"

D. Rejoicing is an act of the will.

1. Psalm 9:2 says, "*I will* be glad and rejoice in thee: *I will* sing praise to thy name, O thou most High."

2. Psalm 20:5 say, "*We will* rejoice in thy salvation, and in the name of our God *we will* set up our banners: the LORD fulfil all thy petitions."

3. Psalm 33:21 says, "For our *heart shall* rejoice in him, because we have trusted in his holy name

4. Psalm says 35:9 says, "And my *soul shall* be joyful in the LORD: *it shall* rejoice in his salvation."

E. The righteous are instructed to *exceedingly* rejoice and be glad.

1. Psalm 68:3 says, "But let the righteous be glad; let them rejoice before God: yea, let them exceedingly rejoice."

2. II Corinthians 7:13 says, "Therefore we were comforted in your comfort: yea, and exceedingly the more joyed we for the joy of Titus, because his spirit was refreshed by you all."

F. Your soul will be involved with true praise.

1. Psalm 35:9 says, "And my soul shall be joyful in the LORD: it shall rejoice in his salvation."

2. A soul is the essence of life manifested in thinking, willing, and knowing. It is our moral and emotional nature, and the seat of real life, vitality, or action. It is the spirit of the human.

G. Those who seek the LORD are to rejoice.

1. Psalm 70:4 says, "Let all those that seek thee rejoice and be glad in thee: and let such as love thy salvation say continually, Let God be magnified."

2. Psalm 105:3 says, "Glory ye in his holy name: let the heart of them rejoice that seek the LORD."

H. The Bible instructs us to make a joyful noise.

1. Psalm 100:1 says, "Make a joyful noise unto the LORD, all ye lands."

2. Psalm 66:1 says, "Make a joyful noise unto God, all ye lands:"

3. Psalm 81:1 says, "Sing aloud unto God our strength: make a joyful noise unto the God of Jacob."

4. Psalm 95:1-2 says "O come let us sing unto the LORD: let us make a joyful noise to the rock of our salvation."

5. Psalm 98:4 says, "Make a joyful noise unto the LORD, all the earth: make a loud noise, and rejoice, and sing praise."

I. Rejoice in the LORD and His glory.

1. Romans 5:2 says, "By whom also we have access by faith into this grace therein we stand, and rejoice in hope of the glory of God."

2. Philippians 3:1 says, "Finally, my brethren, rejoice in the LORD. To write the same things to you, to me indeed is not grievous, but for you it is safe."

3. Philippians 4:4 says, "Rejoice in the Lord always: and again I say, Rejoice."

J. As stated in *Women of the Spirit Bible Study* Volume III, the definition of the words *joy* and *rejoice* are the following:

1. Joy means gladness or delight; to rejoice.

2. Rejoice means to *feel* joy or great delight.

3. Matthew Henry says joy is a constant delight in God.

Lesson II Quiz

1.   Write from memory the following scriptures:

    a.   *Psalm 5:11*:

    b.   *Psalm 33:1*:

    c.   *Psalm 105:3*:

    d.   *Philippians 4:4*:

2.   Rejoicing is an act of the will. Give scriptures to prove this.

    a.

    b.

3.   Give definitions of the following words:

    a.   *Comely:*

    b.   *Upright:*

    c.   *Rejoice*:

4.   The soul is involved in true praise. Give definition of the soul.

5.   Give scriptures that instruct us to make a joyful noise.

    a.

    b.

Women of the Spirit Bible Study

Ablaze With Praise

Lesson III

III. ABLAZE WITH PRAISE

A. Praise the Lord with a whole heart.

1. Psalm 9:1 says, "I will praise thee, O Lord, with my whole heart; I will show forth all thy marvellous works."

2. Psalm 86:12 says, "I will praise thee, O Lord my God, with all my heart: and I will glorify thy name for evermore."

3. Psalm 111:1 says, "PRAISE ye the LORD. I will praise the LORD with my whole heart, in the assembly of the upright, and in the congregation."

4. Psalm 138:1 says, "I will praise thee with my whole heart: before the gods will I sing praise unto thee."

B. Triumphantly praise Him by clapping and lifting your hands.

1. Psalm 47:1 says, "O CLAP your hands, all ye people; shout unto God with the voice of triumph."

2. Psalm 63:4 says, "Thus will I bless thee, while I live: I will lift up my hands in thy name."

3. Psalm 134:1-2 says, "BEHOLD, bless ye the LORD, all ye servants of the LORD, which by night stand in the house of the LORD."

4. Psalm 141:2 says, "Let my prayer be set forth before thee as incense; and the lifting up of my hands as the evening sacrifice."

C. Praise Him by DANCING and leaping!

1. Psalm 149:3 says, "Let them praise his name in the dance: let them sing praises unto him with the timbrel and harp."

2. Psalm 30:11-12 says, "Thou hast turned for me my mourning into dancing: thou hast put off my sackcloth, and girded me with gladness; To the end that my glory may sing praise to thee, and not be silent. O LORD my God, I will give thanks unto thee for ever."

3. Acts 3:8 says, "And he leaping up stood, and walked and entered with them into the temple, walking, and leaping and praising God."

D. All of creation declares the glory of God and is ablaze with praise for their Creator.

1. Psalm 19:1 says, "THE HEAVENS declare the glory of God; and the firmament showeth his handiwork."

2. Because of the rain, "... the little hills rejoice on every side" (Psalm 65:12).

3. Because the pastures are covered with flocks and the valleys with corn, "...They shout for joy, they also sing." (Psalm 65:13).

4. Psalm 89:5 says, "And the heavens shall praise thy wonders, O LORD: thy faithfulness also in the congregaton of the saints."

5. Psalm 69:34 says, "Let the heaven and earth praise him, the seas, and every thing that moveth therein."

6. Psalm 96:11-12 says, "Let the heavens rejoice, and let the earth be glad; let the sea roar, and the fulness thereof. Let the field be joyful, and all that is therein: then shall all the trees of the wood rejoice."

7. Psalm 97:1 says, "The LORD reigneth; let the earth rejoice; let the multitude of isles be glad thereof."

8. Psalm 98:7-8 says, "Let the sea roar, and the fulness thereof; the world, and they that dwell therein. Let the hills be joyful together."

E. *Every* part of *every*one is to bless the Lord.

1. Psalm 103:1 says, "BLESS the LORD, O my soul: and all that is within me, bless his holy name."

2. Read Psalm 103: 20-22:

   a. *Verse 20:* "Bless the LORD, ye his angels, that excel in strength, that do his commandments, hearkening unto the voice of his word."

   b. "Bless ye the LORD, all ye his hosts; ye ministers of his, that do his pleasure."

   c. "Bless the LORD, all his works in all places of his dominion: bless the LORD, O my soul."

3. Psalm 104:1 says, "BLESS the LORD, O my soul. O LORD my God, thou art very great; thou art clothed with honour and majesty.

4. Psalm 66:8 says, "O bless our God, ye people, and make the voice of his praise to be heard."

F.   See the following definition of intense praise:

1.   *Intense* praise is profoundly earnest or intent, characterized by or expressive of strong emotion.

2.   The opposite would be insipid praise, which is dull, flat, and *lacking* in spirit or animation.

Lesson III Quiz

1. Write from memory the following scriptures:

    a. *Psalm 9:1:*

    b. *Psalm 86:12:*

    c. *Psalm 103:1:*

2. Give scriptural references that instruct us to clap and lift our hands unto the Lord.

    a.

    b.

3. Give scriptural references that refer to dancing and leaping.

    a.

    b.

4. What is intense praise? What is the opposite of intense praise?

    a.

    b.

5. Give scriptural references that refers to creation praising the Lord.

    a.

    b.

I Will Yet Praise Him

Lesson IV

36

IV. I WILL YET PRAISE HIM

A.   Praise is not based on the emotions of a woman, but upon the *object* of praise, which is God.

    1.   Yet means nevertheless, or in spite of the situation.

    2.   God is perfect, glorious, mighty, compassionate, and kind. He has done no wrong. Why should He be derived of praise because of our predicament or problem?

    3.   The bigger the problem, the bigger the praise should be.

B.   When trouble surrounds you, praise Him anyway.

    1.   Psalm 71:14 says, "But I will hope continually, and will yet praise thee more and more."

    2.   Acts 16:25 demonstrates how Paul and Silas praised God in prison while their backs were bleeding.

    3.   Habbakuk 3:18 says, "Yet I will rejoice in the LORD, I will joy in the God of my salvation."

4. Verse 17 indicates that there was nothing in which to rejoice.

    a. There were no blossoms on the fig tree.

    b. There was no fruit on the vines.

    c. The olive tree failed.

    d. The fields yielded no meat.

    e. There were no flocks in the stall.

    f. It was a bleak, dismal and hopeless situation, but inspite of what appeared to be a disaster, he rejoiced in the God of his salvation.

C. When your soul is cast down and hope is gone, you should praise Him anyway. This is emphasized three times in two chapters back to back.

    1. Psalm 42:5 says, "Why art thou cast down, O my soul? and why art thou disquieted in me? Hope thou in God: for I shall yet praise him for the help of his countenance."

    2. Psalm 42:11 says, "Why art thou cast down, O my soul? and why art thou disquieted within me? hope thou in God: for I shall yet praise him, who is the health of my countenance, and my God."

    3. Psalm 43:5 says, "Why art thou cast down, O my soul? and why art thou disquieted within me? hope in God: for I shall yet praise him, who is the health of my countenance, and my God."

D.   When you are feeling emotional pain, praise the Lord in spite of the hurt.

    1.   On the day of Hannah's biggest sacrifice, she praised the Lord.

    2.   When she had to give Samuel to the Priest at a young age, she must have shed many tears.

    3.   Read Hannah's prayer in I Samuel 2:1-2, 8-10. "AND HANNAH prayed, and said, My heart rejoiceth in the LORD, mine horn is exalted in the LORD: my mouth is enlarged over mine enemies; because I rejoice in thy salvation. There is none holy as the LORD: for there is none beside thee: neither is there any rock like our God." verses 8-10 say, "He raiseth up the poor out of the dust, and lifteth up the beggar from the dunghill, to set them among princes, and to make them inherit the throne of glory: for the pillars of the earth are the LORD's and he hath set the world upon them. He will keep the feet of his saints, and the wicked shall be silent in darkness; for by strength shall no man prevail. The adversaries of the LORD shall be broken to pieces; out of heaven shall he thunder upon them: the LORD shall judge the ends of the earth; and he shall give strength unto his king, and exalt the horn of his anointed."

E.   There is no situation that should keep you from praising Him. We must praise Him in all things.

    1.   Ephesians 5:19-20 says, "Speaking to yourselves in psalms and hymns and spiritual songs, singing and making melody in your heart to the Lord; Giving thanks **always** for **all** things unto God and the Father in the name of our Lord Jesus Christ."

3.   Read Philippians 4:6.

   a.   "Be careful for nothing; but in *every* thing by prayer and supplication with *thanksgiving* let your requests be made known to God."

   b.   We are instructed to thank Him, even when we are in need and asking for something. Nothing is to be taken for granted, but the Lord is to be thanked and praised for *every* thing.

Lesson IV Quiz

1.   Praise should be based upon what?

2.   Write from memory the following scriptures:

    a.   *Psalm 71:14:*

    b.   *Habbakuk 3:18:*

    c.   *Psalm 42:5:*

    d.   *Ephesians 5:19-20:*

    e.   *I Thessalonians 5:18:*

    f.   *Philippians 4:6:*

3.   Give definition of *yet*.

4.   We are to praise God when our soul is cast down. Give scriptural reference.

Women of the Spirit Bible Study

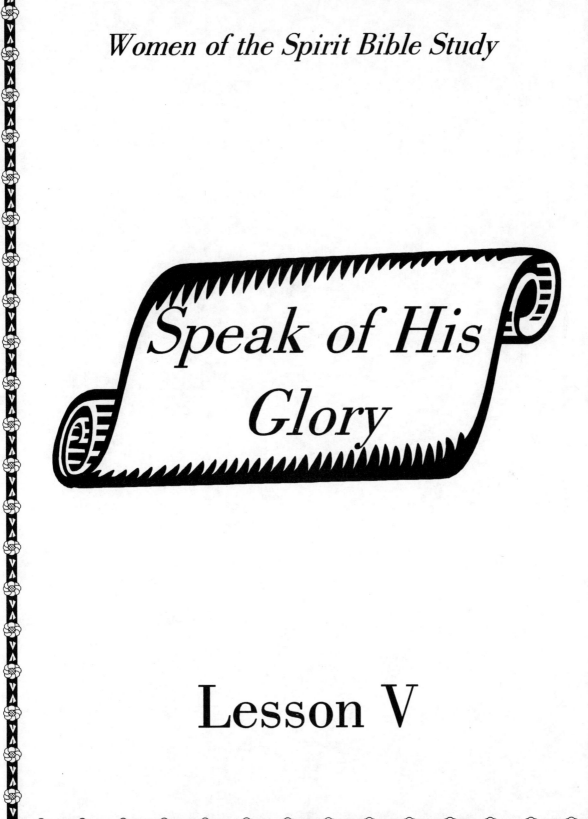

Speak of His Glory

Lesson V

V. SPEAK OF HIS GLORY

A.   We must tell future generations about His mighty acts.

    1.   Read Psalm 145:4-7:

        a.   *Verse 4* says, "One generation shall praise thy works to another, and shall declare thy mighty acts."

        b.   *Verse 5* says, "I will *speak* of the glorious honour of thy majesty, and of thy wondrous works."

        c.   *Verse 6* says, "And men shall *speak* of the might of thy terrible acts: and I will *declare* thy greatness."

        d.   *Verse 7* says, "They shall *abundantly utter* the memory of thy great goodness, and *shall sing* of thy righteousness."

    2.   Read Psalm 145:10-12:

        a.   *Verse 10* says, "All thy works shall praise thee, O LORD; and thy saints shall bless thee."

      b.   *Verse 11* says, "They shall *speak* of the glory of thy kingdom, and *talk* of thy power;"

      c.   *Verse 12* says, "To *make known* to the sons of men his mighty acts, and the glorious majesty of his kingdom."

   3.   Psalm 145:21 says, "My mouth shall speak the praise of the LORD: and let all flesh bless his holy name for ever and ever."

   4.   Psalm 45:17 says, "I will make thy name to be remembered in all generations: therefore shall the people praise thee for ever and ever."

   5.   Psalm 71:24 says, "My tongue also shall talk of thy righteousness all the day long; for they are confounded, for they are brought unto shame, that seek my hurt."

B.   A woman's mouth always should be filled with praise.

   1.   Psalm 71:8 says, "Let my mouth be filled with thy praise and with thy honour *all* the day."

   2.   Psalm 35:28 says, "And my tongue shall speak of thy righteousness and of thy praise *all* the day long."

   3.   Psalm 63:3 says, "Because thy lovingkindness is better than life, my lips shall praise thee."

C.   Speak not your fears, but magnify the LORD.

   1.   When Mary went to visit her cousin Elisabeth after her visitation with the angel, Gabriel, she did not say, "I'm so afraid of the future. I don't know exactly what it entails." Instead, she magnified the Lord.

2.   Luke 1:46-55 is her prayer.
"And Mary said, My soul doth magnify the Lord. And my spirit hath rejoiced in God my Savious. For he hath regarded the low state of his handmaiden: for, behold, from henceforth all generations shall call me blessed. For he that is mighty hath done to me great things; and holy is his name. And his mercy is on them that fear him from generation to generation. He hath shown strength with his arm; he hath scattered the proud in the imagination of their hearts. He hath put down the mighty from their seats, and exalted them of low degree. He hath filled the hungry with good things; and the rich he hath sent empty away. He hath helped his servant Israel, in remembrace of his mercy; As he spake to our fathers to Abraham, and to his seed for ever."

D.   The Lord is writing a book of remembrance for those who fear Him, think upon His name, and speak of His glory.

1.   Malachi 3:16 says, "Then they that feared the LORD spake often one to another and the LORD hearkened, and heard it, and a book of remembrance was written before him for them that thought upon his name."

2.   Malachi 3:17, "And they shall be mine, saith the LORD of hosts, in that day when I make up my jewels; and I will spare them, as a man spareth his own son that serveth him."

E.   The angels speak of His glory, and instruct us to worship God.

1.   Luke 2:13-14 says, "And suddenly there was with the angel a multitude of the heavenly host praising God, and saying, Glory to God in the highest, and on earth peace, good will toward men."

2.   Revelation 22:9 says, "Then saith he unto me, See thou do it not: for I am thy fellowservant, and of thy brethren the prophets, and of them which keep the sayings of this book: worship God."

F.   The shepherds and early Christians spoke of His glory.

    1.   Luke 2:20 says, "And the shepherds returned, glorifying and praising God for all the things that they had heard and and seen, as it was told unto them."

    2.   Luke 2:38 says, "And she coming in that instant gave thanks likewise unto the Lord and spake of him to all them that looked for redemption in Jerusalem."

    3.   Acts 4:18-20 says, "And they called them, and commanded them not to speak at all nor teach in the name of Jesus. But Peter and John answered and said unto them, Whether it be right in the sight of God to hearken unto you more than unto God, judge ye. For we cannot but speak the things which we have seen and heard."

Lesson V Quiz

1. We are not to speak our _____, but are to _____ the Lord.

2. The Lord is writing a _____ of _____ for all those who think upon His _____ and _____ of His _____.

3. Write from memory the following scriptures:

    a. *Psalm 45:17:*

    b. *Psalm 71:8:*

    c. *Malachi 3:16:*

    d. *Luke 2:13-14:*

4. To whom should we speak of his glory?

5. What did Mary do when she received news that she would be the mother of Jesus?

Women of the Spirit Bible Study

Infinite Praise

Lesson VI

VI. INFINITE PRAISE

A. Infinite means, without end, boundless, immeasurable, numerous, and vast.

    1. Praise cannot be measured out with stinginess.

    2. It must always be without end. You must praise incessantly.

B. We are to praise Him all the day, everyday.

    1. Psalm 145:2 says, "*Every day* will I bless thee; and I will praise thy name for ever and ever."

    2. Psalm 89:16 says, "In thy name shall they rejoice *all the day*: and in thy righteousness shall they be exalted."

    3. Psalm 35:28 says, "And my tongue shall speak of thy righteousness and of thy praise *all the day long*."

C. We are to praise Him and bless His name continually.

    1. Luke 24:53 says, "And were *continually* in the temple, praising and blessing God. Amen."

2. Psalm 71:6 says, "By thee have I been holden up from the womb: thou art he that took me out of my mother's bowels: my praise shall be *continually* of thee."

3. Psalm 35:27 says, "Let them shout for joy, and be glad, that favour my righteous cause: yea, let them say *continually*, Let the LORD be magnified, which hath pleasure in the prosperity of his servant."

4. Psalm 34:1 says, "I WILL bless the LORD at all times: his praise shall *continually* be in my mouth."

D. We are to praise Him forever.

1. Psalm 89:1 says, "I WILL sing of the mercies of the LORD *for ever*: with my mouth will I make known thy faithfulness to all generations."

2. Psalm 145:1 says, "I will extol thee, my God, O king; and I will bless thy name *for ever and ever*."

3. Psalm 52:9 says, "I will praise thee *for ever*, because thou hast done it: and I will wait on thy name; for it is good before thy saints."

4. Psalm 115:17-18 says, "The dead praise not the LORD, neither any that go down into silence. But we will bless the LORD from this time forth and *for ever more*. Praise the LORD."

E. His kingdom is everlasting. Our praise should be everlasting.

1. Psalm 106:48 says, "Blessed be the LORD God of Israel from *everlasting to everlasting*: and let all the people say, Amen. Praise ye the LORD."

2. Psalm 90:2 says, "Before the mountains were brought forth, or ever thou hadst formed the earth and the world, even from *everlasting to everlasting*, thou art God."

3. Psalm 93:1-2 says, "THE LORD reigneth, he is clothed with majesty; the LORD is clothed with strength, wherewith he hath girded himself: the world also is established, that it cannot be moved. Thy throne is established of old: thou art from *everlasting*."

F. All the earth and nations are to praise Him.

1. Psalm 66:4 says, "All the *earth* shall worship thee, and shall sing unto thee; they shall sing to thy name. Selah."

2. Psalm 22:27 says, "All the ends of the world shall remember and turn unto the LORD: and all the kindreds of the *nations* shall worship before thee."

3. Psalm 148:2-5 says, "Praise ye him, all his angels: praise ye him, all his hosts. praise ye him, sun and moon: praise him, all ye stars of light. Praise him, ye waters that be above the heavens. Let them praise the name of the LORD: for he commanded, and they were created."

4. Psalm 148:7-13 says, "Praise the LORD from the *earth*, ye dragons, and all deeps: Fire, and hail; snow, and vapour; stormy wind fulfilling his word: Mountains, and all hills; fruitful trees, and all cedars: beasts, and all cattle; creeping things; and flying fowls: Kings of the *earth*, and all people; princes, and all judges of the *earth*: Both young men, and maidens; old men, and children: let them praise the name of the LORD: for his name alone is excellent: his glory is above the earth and heaven."

G.   Praise will be in the mouth of those who triumph over the beast, as shown in Revelation 15:2-4.

   1.   Revelation 15:2 says, "And I saw as it were a sea of glass mingled with fire: and them that had gotten the victory over the beast, and over his image, and over his mark, and over the number of his name, stand on the sea of glass, having the harps of God."

   2.   Revelation 15:3 says, "And they sing the song of Moses the servant of God, and the song of the Lamb, saying Great and marvellous are thy works, Lord God Almighty; just and true are thy ways, thou King of saints."

   3.   Revelation 15:4 says, "Who shall not fear thee, O Lord, and glorify thy name? for thou only art holy: for all nations shall come and worship before thee; for thy judgments are made manifest."

   4.   Revelations 15:8 says, "And the temple was filled with smoke from the glory of God, and from his power; and no man was able to enter into the temple, till the seven plagues of the seven angels were fulfilled."

H.   Praise surrounds the throne of God.

   1.   Please read Revelation 19:1, 3-7.

      a.   *Verse 1*: "AND AFTER these things I heard a great voice of much people in heaven, saying, Alleluia; Salvation, and glory, and honour, and power, unto the Lord our God:"

      b.   *Verse 3*: "And again they said, Alleluia. And her smoke rose up for ever and ever."

      c.   *Verse 4*: "And the four and twenty elders and the four beasts fell down and worshipped God that sat on the throne, saying, Amen; Alleluia."

d.   *Verse 5*: "And a voice came out of the throne, saying , Praise our God, all ye his servants, praise our God, all ye his sevants, and ye that fear him, both small and great."

e.   *Verse 6*: "And I heard as it were the voice of a great multitude, and as the voice of many waters, and as the voice of mighty thunderings, saying, Alleluia: for the Lord God omnipotent reigneth."

f.   *Verse 7*: "Let us be glad and rejoice, and give honour to him; for the marriage of the Lamb is come, and his wife hath made herself ready."

g.   *Note*: As praise surrounds the throne of God in heaven, so must praise surround our heart's throne.

2.   Please read Revelation 4:6-11.

a.   *Verse 6*: "And before the throne there was a sea of glass like unto crystal: and in the midst of the throne, and round about the throne, were four beasts full of eyes before and behind."

b.   *Verse 7*: "And the first beast was like a lion, and the second beast like a calf, and the third beast had a face as a man, and the fourth beast was like a flying eagle."

c.   *Verse 8*: "And the four beasts had each of them six wings about him; and they were full of eyes within: and thy rest not day and night, saying, Holy, holy, holy, Lord God Almighty, which was, and is, and is to come."

d.   *Verse 9*: "And when those beasts give glory and honour and thanks to him that sat on the throne, who liveth for ever and ever."

e.   *Verse 10*: "The four and twenty elders fall down before him that sat on the throne, and worship him that liveth for ever and ever, and cast their crowns before the throne, saying."

f.   *Verse 11*: "Thou art worthy, O Lord, to receive glory and honour and power: for thou hast created all things, and for the pleasure they are and were created."

3.   Revelation 5:11-12 says, "And I beheld, and I heard the voice of many angels round about the throne and the beasts and the elders: and the number of them was ten thousand times ten thousand and thousands of thousands. Saying with a loud voice, Worthy is the Lamb that was slain to receive power, and riches, and wisdom, and strength, honour, and glory, and blessing."

I.   We will all worship Him and every knee shall bow before Him.

1.   Isaiah 45:22-23 says, "Look unto me, and be ye saved, all the ends of the earth: for I am God, and there is none else. I have sworn by myself, the word is gone out of my mouth in righteousness, and shall not return, that unto me every knee shall bow, every tongue shall swear."

2.   Philippians 2:10-11 says, "That at the name of Jesus every knee should bow, of things in heaven, and things in earth, and things under the earth: And that every tongue should confess that Jesus Christ is Lord, to the glory of God the Father."

Lesson VI Quiz

1.   Give definition of infinite.

2.   Give scriptural references that says we are to praise Him everyday.

   a.

   b.

3.   Give scriptural references that says we are to praise Him continually.

   a.

   b.

4.   Write from memory the following Scriptures:

   a.   *Psalm 34:1:*

   b.   *Psalm 145:2:*

   c.   *Psalm 35:27:*

   d.   *Philippians 2:10-11:*

5.   Give scriptural references that says we are to praise Him forever.

   a.

   b.

6.   _____ surrounds the throne of God.

New Song of Praise

Lesson VII

VII. NEW SONG OF PRAISE

A. The Lord gives His people a new song. We are constantly instructed to sing songs unto the Lord.

1. Psalm 40:3 says, "And he hath put a new song in my mouth, even praise unto our God: many shall see it, and fear, and shall trust in the LORD."

2. Psalm 149:1 says, "PRAISE ye the LORD, Sing unto the LORD a new song, and his praise in the congregation of saints."

3. Psalm 33:3 says, "Sing unto him a new song; play skillfully with a loud noise."

4. Psalm 96:1-2 says, "O SING unto the LORD a new song: sing unto the LORD, all the earth. Sing unto the LORD, bless his name; show forth his salvation from day to day."

5. Psalm 30:4 says, "Sing unto the LORD, O ye saints of his, and give thanks at the remembrance of his holiness."

6. Psalm 105:2 says, "Sing unto him, sing psalms unto him: talk ye of all his wondrous works."

7. Ephesians 5:19 says, "Speaking to yourselves in psalms and hymns and spiritual songs, singing and making melody in your heart to the Lord;"

8. Colossians 3:16 says, "Let the word of Christ dwell in you richly in all wisdom; teaching and admonishing one another in psalms and hymns and spiritual songs, singing with grace in your hearts to the Lord."

9. Psalm 68:32 says, "Sing unto God, ye kingdoms of the earth; O sing praises unto the Lord; Selah:"

10. Isaiah 42:10 says, "Sing unto the LORD a new song, and praise from the end of the earth, ye that go down to the sea, and all that is therein; the isles, and inhabitants thereof."

11. Read Revelation 14:2-3.

   a. *Verse 2* says, "And I heard a voice from heaven, as the voice of many waters, and as the voice of a great thunder: and I heard the voice of harpers harping with their harps:

   b. *Verse 3 says,* "And they sung as it were a new song before the throne, and before the four beasts, and the elders: and no man could learn that song but the hundred and forty and four thousand, which were redeemed from the earth."

B. Christians are instructed to come before His presence with thanksgiving and singing.

   1. Psalm 100:2 says, "Serve the LORD with gladness: come before his presence with singing."

   2. Psalm 147:7 says, "Sing unto the LORD with thanksgiving; sing praise upon the harp unto our God."

C.   Sing to the Lord because of His blessings.

    1.   Psalm 13:6 says, "I will sing unto the LORD, because he hath dealt bountifully with me."

    2.   Read Psalm 59:16-17.

        a.   *Verse 16* says, "But I will sing of the power; yea, I will sing aloud of thy mercy in the morning: for thou hast been my defence and refuge in the day of my trouble."

        b.   *Verse 17* says, "Unto thee, O my strength will I sing: for God is my defence, and the God of my mercy."

D.   Your heart must be fixed in its purpose to praise the Lord. You must have an *I will* or *I shall* attitude and a made up mind.

    1.   Psalm 57:1 says, "BE MERCIFUL unto me, O God, be mericful unto me: for my soul trusteth in thee: yea, in the shadow of the wings *will I* make my refuge until these calamities be overpast."

    2.   Psalm 27:6 says, "And now shall mine head be lifted up above mine enemies round about me: therefore will I offer in his tabernacle sacrifices of joy; *I will* sing, yea, *I will* sing praises unto the LORD."

    3.   Psalm 104:33 says, "*I will* sing unto the LORD as long as I live: *I will* sing praise to my God while I have my being."

    4.   Read Psalm 108:1,3.

        a.   *Verse 1* says, "O GOD, my heart is fixed; *I will* sing and give praise, even with my glory."

    b. *Verse 3* says, "*I will* praise thee, O LORD, among the people: and *I will* sing praises unto thee among the nations."

F. We must sing about the Lord's glory and His wondrous, mighty acts, and share them with people.

  1. Psalm 9:1 says, "I WILL praise thee, O LORD, with my whole heart; I will show forth all thy marvellous works."

  2. Psalm 105:1-2 says, "O GIVE thanks unto the LORD; call upon his name: make known his deeds among the people. Sing unto him, sing psalms unto him: talk ye of all his wondrous works."

G. His people are to sing praises to His **name**.

  1. Psalm 68:4 says, "Sing unto God, sing praises to his name: extol him that rideth upon the heavens by his name JAH, and rejoice before him."

    a. JAH is an abbreviation for Jehovah.

    b. Exodus 6:3 "And I appeared unto Abraham, unto Isaac, and unto Jacob, by the name of God Almighty, but by my name JEHOVAH was I not known to them."

  2. Psalm 7:17 says, 'I will praise the LORD according to his righteousness: and will sing praise to the name of the LORD most high."

  3. Psalm 8:1 says, "O LORD our Lord, how excellent is thy name in all the earth! who hast set thy glory above the heavens."

  4. Psalm 69:30 says, "I will praise the name of God with a song, and will magnify him with thanksgiving."

H.   Sing when you feel as if you are surrounded by the enemy.

1.   When Jehosaphat was outnumbered by heathen armies, he fasted, prayed, and sought God for an answer. The answer came: he was to sing his way to victory!

2.   II Chronicles 20:21-22 says, "And when he had consulted with the people, he appointed singers unto the LORD, and that should praise the beauty of holiness, as they went out before the army, and to say, Praise the LORD; for his mercy endureth for ever. And when they began to sing and to praise, the LORD set ambushments against the children of Ammon, Moab, and mount Seir, which were come against Judah; and they were smitten."

Lesson VII Quiz

1.   Write from memory the following scriptures:

   a.   *Psalm 40:3:*

   b.   *Psalm 100:2:*

   c.   *Ephesians 5:19:*

   d.   *Colossians 3:16:*

   e.   *Psalm 13:6:*

   f.   *Psalm 108:1:*

   g.   *Psalm 9:1:*

   h.   *Psalm 8:1:*

2.   Give scriptural references that instructs God's people to sing a new song.

   a.

   b.

   c.

3.   How are we to come before His presence?

4.   Give an example of what you are to do when you feel as if you **are**
     surrounded by the enemy.

5.   Your heart must be _____ in its _____ to
     _____ the Lord.

Women of the Spirit Bible Study

Greatly to be Praised

Lesson VIII

VIII.   GREATLY TO BE PRAISED

A.   The Lord is awesome and greatly to be praised!

    1.   Psalm 145:3 says, "Great is the LORD, and greatly to be praised; and his greatness is unsearchable."

    2.   Psalm 48:1 says, "GREAT IS the LORD, and greatly to be praised in the city of our God, in the mountain of his holiness."

    3.   Psalm 96:4 says, "For the LORD is great, and greatly to be praised: he is to be feared above all gods."

    4.   I Chronicles 16:25 says, "For great is the LORD, and greatly to be praised : he also is to be feared above all gods."

B.   God helps His people. They should greatly rejoice.

    1.   Psalm 28:7 says, "The LORD is my strength and my shield; my heart trusted in him, and I am helped: therefore my heart greatly rejoiceth; and with my song will I praise him."

2.   Isaiah 61:10 says, "I will greatly rejoice in the LORD, my soul shall be joyful in my God; for he hath clothed me with the garments for salvation, he hath covered me with the robe of righteousness, as a bridegroom decketh himself with ornaments, and as a bride adorneth herself with her jewels."

C.   Christians should have not only have an *I will* attitude, but also have an *I will greatly praise* attitude.

1.   Psalm 109:30 says, "*I will greatly praise* the LORD with my mouth; yea I will praise him among the multitude."

2.   Psalm 71:23 says, "My lips *shall greatly rejoice* when I sing unto thee; and my soul, which thou hast redeemed."

D.   God's people should make their boast in the Lord.

1.   Psalm 34:2 says, "My soul shall make her boast in the LORD: the humble shall hear thereof, and be glad."

2.   Psalm 44:8 says, "In God we boast all the day long, and praise thy name for ever. Selah."

E.   Exalt His name and magnify the LORD.

1.   Psalm 34:3 says, "O magnify the LORD with me, and let us exalt his name together."

2.   Psalm 18:46 says, "The LORD liveth; and blessed be my rock; and let the God of my salvation be exalted."

3.   Psalm 21:13 says, "Be thou exalted, Lord, in thine own strength: so will we sing and praise thy power."

4.   Psalm 57:5,11 both say, "Be thou exalted, O God, above the heavens; let thy glory be above all the earth."

5.	Psalm 107:32 says, "Let them exalt him also in the congregation of the people and praise him in the assembly of the elders."

6.	Read Psalm 99:2,3,5, and 9.

    a.	*Verse 2* says, "The LORD is great in Zion; and he is high above all the people."

    b.	*Verse 3* says, "Let them praise thy great and terrible name; for it is holy."

    c.	*Verse 5* says, "Exalt ye the LORD our God, and worship at his footstool; for he is holy."

    d.	*Verse 9* says, "Exalt the LORD our God, and worship at his holy hill; for the LORD our God is holy."

7.	Psalm 118:28 says, "Thou art my God, and I will praise thee: thou art my God, I will exalt thee."

8.	Psalm 30:1 says, "I will exalt thee, O LORD: for thou hast lifted me up, and hast not made my foes to rejoice over me."

9.	Psalm 108:5 says, "Be thou exalted, O God, above the heavens: and the glory above all the earth."

F.	Make His praise glorious and give Him glory in all things.

1.	Psalm 66:2 says, "Sing forth the honour of his name: make his praise glorious."

2.	Psalm 29:1 says, "GIVE UNTO the LORD, O ye mighty, give unto the LORD glory and strength."

3. I Chronicles 16:28 says, "Give unto the LORD, ye kindreds of the people, give unto the LORD glory and strength."

4. Isaiah 42:8 says, "I am the LORD: that is my name: and my glory will I not give to another, neither my praise to graven images."

5. Isaiah 42:12 says, "Let them give glory unto the LORD, and declare his praise in the islands."

6. Revelation 14:7 says, "Saying with a loud voice, Fear God, and give glory to him; for the hour of his judgment is come: and worship him that made heaven, and earth, and the sea, and the fountains of waters."

G. God's children are instructed to praise Him with instruments.

1. Psalm 33:2 says, "Praise the LORD with harp: sing unto him with the psaltery and an instrument of ten strings."

2. Psalm 68:25 says, "The singers went before, the players on instruments followed after; among them were the damsels playing with timbrels."

3. Psalm 71:22 says, "I will also praise thee with the psaltery, even thy truth, O my God: unto thee will I sing with the harp, O thou Holy One of Israel."

4. Psalm 98:5 says, 'Sing unto the LORD with the harp; with the harp, and the voice of a psalm."

5. Psalm 98:6 says, "With trumpets and sound of cornet make a joyful noise before the LORD, the King."

6. Psalm 87:7 says, "As well the singers as the players on instruments shall be there: all my springs are in thee."

7.   Read Psalm 92:1,3.

      a.   *Verse 1* says: "It is a good thing to give thanks unto the LORD, and to sing praises unto thy name, O most High:"

      b.   *Verse 3* says, "Upon an instrument of ten strings, and upon the psaltery; upon the harp with a solemn sound."

Lesson VIII Quiz

1. Give scriptural references that instruct everyone to greatly praise the Lord.

   a.

   b.

2. Write from memory the following scriptures:

   a.   *Psalm 34:3:*

   b.   *Psalm 21:13:*

   c.   *Isaiah 42:8:*

3. Make his _____ _____ and give Him _____ in all things.

4. Exalt his _____ and _____ the LORD.

5. Give scriptures that instruct His people to praise Him on the instruments.

   a.

   b.

   c.

Epilogue

Psalm 150

"PRAISE YE the LORD. Praise God in his Sanctuary: Praise him in the firmament of his power. Praise him for his mighty acts; praise him according to his excellent greatness. Praise him with the sound of the trumpet: Praise him with the psaltery and harp. Praise him with the timbrel and dance: Praise him with stringed instruments and organs. Praise him upon the loud cymbals: Praise him upon the high soundings cymbals. Let everything that hath breath praise the LORD. Praise ye the LORD."

Author's Note:

I want to share with you three interesting pieces of evidence which prove that praise works.

Number 1: a letter I received in the mail. The name and some of the details have been deleted for the sake of privacy, but the letter remains the same–unedited.

Dear Sister Haney,

I read your *Women of the Spirit Bible Study, Vol. I Love, God's Way*! I wanted to let you know what a true blessing it has been to me.

I had been separated from my ex-husband 34 months and 2 days, when I started to read the lesson on "Love Your Enemy." For all these months there was so much hate built up inside. My ex-husband and his girlfriend would see me out and laugh at me. I had to leave the comfort of my home for them.

All these things I thought I had overcome through prayer and fasting. But for 4 days I'd be woken out of my sleep for 1 1/2 to 2 hours to pray. On February 21, 1996, I received an awful letter from my ex's girlfriend. She was tearing me down to threads, or should I say <u>trying</u>. That afternoon my next lesson was "Love Your Enemy." I cried and prayed and God opened my eyes through the Word. That night again at 2:37 a.m., I was woken up. But this time it was different-I was rejoicing, there was so much freedom I felt. I had never experienced this kind of forgiveness ever before. I wrote them a letter forgiving them for what they'd done.

I just wanted to say thank you so much for allowing God to inspire and direct you in the writing of this book. Just think if you would not have written it, then I may have still been bound.

Your friend in Christ,

Number 2: An experience.

Recently, I called one of my daughters, (who had been going through a difficult trial in her life), from the airport where I was flying out of that night. She had received some disturbing news that day, and I had told her to praise the Lord in spite of her circumstances. She said, "Mother, the strangest thing happened to me tonight." I asked her what happened, and she proceeded to tell me the following story:

"Tonight on the way home from the Church, I began to praise God for all the things that He was going to bring into my life in the future. I thanked Him for many things, but then I said, 'Thank you, God, for the laughter, giggles, happiness, and joy that you are going to bring to me.'"

She said, "Suddenly, the presence of the Lord came in the car, and I started laughing so hard; it was *belly* laughter, from way down deep. I laughed for two minutes. I never had experienced anything like it before, but I felt so clean. It was an awesome experience, and it let me know that God was hearing my prayer and that He cared about what I was going through. When I started praising Him, He sent laughter to me. It is hard to explain the way I feel, but I will never forget what happened tonight."

Number 3: A dream taken from my book, *Clean Out the Ashes*, told to me by a friend. These were her words:

During a particularly difficult time in our lives, my husband I were on a fast. He was up into the wee hours of the morning praying for me that I might be encouraged. About 3:00 a.m. I was awakened with this vision:

I was looking down from the sky upon a dark and dismal road that a lady was fearfully walking down. The lady was me, and life was dark, uncertain, and very threatening. I could not see anything surrounding me, only the path winding downward before me. All of a sudden the thought came to me that I had nothing to lose and I threw my hands in the air and began to praise and worship God.

Then from across the sky I saw a very angry animal-like face appear, and in its fury it sent bolts of lightning to destroy me. Just as the bolts were about to strike me, a large hand, which I knew to be God's came in front of me with a shield so shiny that when the lightening struck it, the whole sky lit up and there was such beauty around me and rainbow-like colors appeared in the sky. Then I knew the beauty was there all along, it was only the darkness that hid it from my view. What the enemy had intended for evil, the Lord intended for my good."

Women of the Spirit Bible Study

Vol. I: Love, God's Way

Vol. II: Faith, Prayer, & Spiritual Warfare

Vol. III: All About Trials

Vol. IV: Wisdom, Attitudes, & Character

Vol. V: Women of Compassion

Vol. VI: The Power of Praise

These can be ordered from:

Radiant Life Publications
9025 N. West Lane
Stockton, CA 95210
Ph. 209-957-4027
Fax 209-476-7888

The following books by Joy Haney can also be ordered:

Pressed Down But Looking Up	$6.00
The Radiant Woman	5.00
The Elite	5.00
May I Wash Your Feet	5.95
Behold, the Nazarite Woman	5.95
When Ye Pray	6.50
When Ye Fast	5.00
When Ye Give	6.95
The Carpenter	5.95
Great Faith	6.00
Clean Out the Ashes	8.95
Philip's Family	6.00
The Privileged Woman	6.95
What Do You Do When You Don't Feel Like Doing What You're Doing?	7.50
Diamonds for Dusty Roads	8.95
The Dreamers	6.00
The Blessing of the Prison	7.50

New Release in May-1996:

How to have Radiant Health	8.95

New Releases in the Fall-1996:

The Healing Power of Prayer for the Mind & Body
Nothing But the Best: A Call to Excellence

Note: See page 87 for ordering instructions. You may also call phone #209-469-2210.